AUSTRALIA,
THE PACIFIC,
AND ANTARCTICA

Atolls between American Samoa and Tonga

The World in Maps

"AUSTRALIA, THE PACIFIC, AND ANTARCTICA"

Martyn Bramwell

Lerner Publications Company • Minneapolis

**First American edition published in 2000
by Lerner Publications Company**

© 2000 by Graham Beehag Books

Lerner Publications Company
A division of Lerner Publishing Group
241 First Avenue North
Minneapolis, MN 55401 U.S.A.

Website address: www.lernerbooks.com

Library of Congress Cataloging-in-Publication Data

Bramwell, Martyn.
   Australia, the Pacific, and Antarctica / by Martyn Bramwell.
      p. cm. — (The world in maps)
Includes index.
ISBN 0-8225-2917-3 (lib. bdg. : alk. paper)
1. Oceania—Juvenile literature. 2. Oceania—Maps for
children—Juvenile literature. 3. Australia—Juvenile literature.
4. Australia—Maps for children—Juvenile literature. 5. New
Zealand—Juvenile literature. 6. New Zealand—Maps for
children—Juvenile literature. 7. Antarctica—Juvenile literature.
8. Antarctica—Maps for children—Juvenile literature. [1. Oceania.
2. New Zealand. 3. Antarctica.] I. Title. II. Series: Bramwell, Martyn.
The world in maps.
   DU17 .B734 2000
   919—dc21   00-010739

Printed in Singapore by Tat Wei Printing Packaging Pte Ltd
Bound in the United States of America
1 2 3 4 5 6 – OS – 05 04 03 02 01 00

CONTENTS

AUSTRALIA, the PACIFIC, and ANTARCTICA

Three enormous and hugely contrasting regions—Australia, the islands of the Pacific Ocean, and the great southern continent of Antarctica—lie in the Southern Hemisphere. Together they cover 40 percent of the earth's surface, yet between them they have a total population of barely 30 million people.

Australia is the only country to have an entire continent to itself. Separated from other land areas 200 million years ago, Australia became home to a unique collection of animals and plants, many of them found nowhere else on earth. Its original people, the Aborigines, arrived by canoe from Southeast Asia more than 40,000 years ago. These

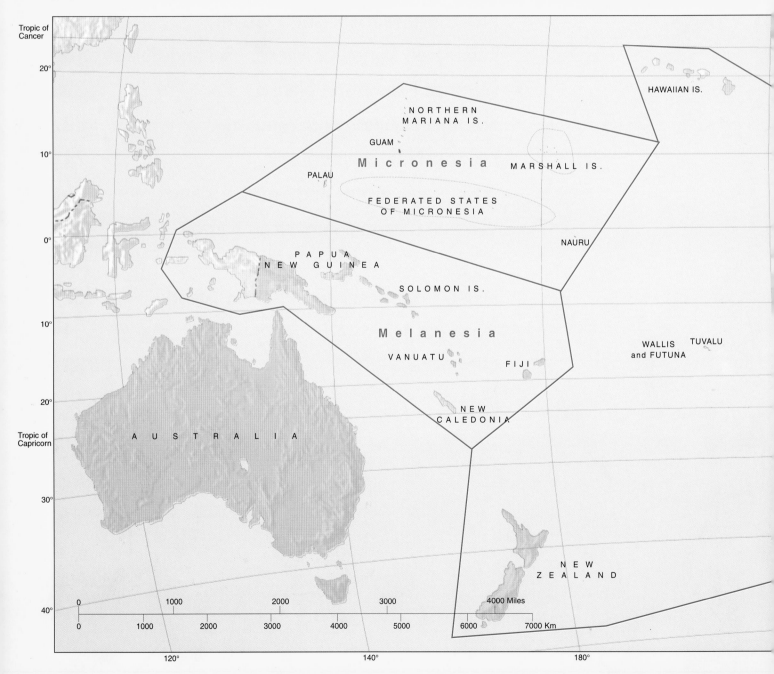

early peoples lived by hunting and gathering. In the 1600s, when Europeans first began to explore the Southern Hemisphere, about 300,000 Aborigines lived in Australia. Britain took control of the continent in the late 1700s, using it first as a place to send convicted criminals. It was not until the 1800s that the British began to explore the country, setting Australia on the road to become a leading industrialized nation.

The Pacific Ocean covers more of the earth's surface than all the world's land areas combined. It stretches more than 14,500 miles, from the islands of Malaysia in the west to the coast of Colombia in the east and from the Bering Sea off Alaska's shores in the north to the icy waters of Antarctica in the south. Almost lost within this vast expanse are between 20,000 and 30,000 islands—the exact number is unknown. Thousands are tiny coral islands and reefs that hardly break the ocean surface. Others, such as New Guinea and New Zealand, are among the world's largest islands. Scattered across the ocean—alone or in clusters or in beadlike chains—the Pacific islands are home to a remarkable variety of peoples. Geographers divide the islands into three groups. Melanesia, meaning "black islands," includes New Guinea, the Solomons, New Caledonia, Fiji, and Vanuatu. To the north lies Micronesia (small islands), including Guam, the Marshall Islands, the Caroline Islands, Nauru, and others. And to the east stretches Polynesia (many islands), a group that extends north to south from Hawaii to New Zealand and west to east from Tuvalu to Easter Island.

Antarctica has no people, apart from a few thousand visiting scientists, and no year-round animal residents. In summer its shores and offshore islands teem with breeding seabirds, penguins, and seals, but in winter it is almost deserted—a vast, high, windswept **plateau** of snow and ice, broken in places by the jagged peaks of mountain ranges jutting through ice up to two miles thick.

NORTH

PACIFIC

OCEAN

KIRIBATI

P o l y n e s i a

WESTERN
SAMOA

AMERICAN SAMOA

TONGA   COOK IS.   FRENCH
                                            POLYNESIA
NIUE

PITCAIRN I.

SOUTH

PACIFIC

OCEAN

120°

Above: Floodwaters frequently cover the swamp-lined banks of Papua New Guinea's Sepik River, so the local people build their houses on stilts.

Australia

Australia

Status:	Constitutional Monarchy and Federation of States
Area:	2.98 million square miles
Population:	19.0 million
Capital:	Canberra
Language:	English
Currency:	Australian dollar (100 cents)

Australia—the world's sixth largest country—is the only country to occupy an entire continent. It is also one of the most thinly populated countries in the world, with an average of only six people per square mile. But even that figure is misleading. Deserts, scrub, and dry grasslands cover nearly all of western and central Australia, and these arid and semi-arid regions support an average of only one or two people per square mile.

Most of Australia's 19 million people are concentrated along the southern and eastern coasts, where there is enough rainfall to support intensive agriculture and large urban areas. In fact, more than 80 percent of Australians live in cities and towns. Some of the largest cities are Perth in the southwest, Adelaide, Melbourne, and Sydney in the southeast, and Brisbane in the east.

Agriculture and mining are the mainstays of Australia's economy. They employ relatively few people but produce virtually all of Australia's export goods. The two sectors are also the source of raw materials for many of Australia's industries.

About 65 percent of Australia's land is available for farming, but climate and terrain determine how farmers use the land. The western two-thirds of Australia consist of a vast, dry plateau. Deserts, unsuitable for any kind of farming, fill the central region and are surrounded by dry grasslands that extend to the coast. Livestock farmers raise sheep on these grasslands, primarily for their wool, which is one of Australia's principal exports. Rainfall increases toward the southwest, allowing farmers to grow wheat, another important export. A small region south of Perth is wet enough to nurture crops of fruits and vegetables and to support dairy herds. In the northern part of the state of Western Australia, farmers graze herds of beef cattle.

The eastern one-third of Australia divides into two subregions—a central lowland region and the eastern highlands, which parallel the coast from Cape York to Melbourne. Farmers in the southern part of the lowlands raise cattle and sheep and grow wheat, barley, and vegetables.

Right: Ayers Rock—Uluru in the Aboriginal language—rises to 2,844 feet in central Australia. Caves along its flanks contain hundreds of ancient Aboriginal rock paintings.

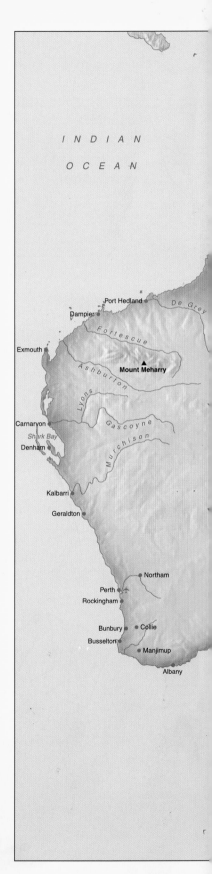

Coral
Sea

Cape York

Weipa

*Princess
Charlotte Bay*

Cooktown

Cairns

Innisfail

Ingham

Townsville
Ayr

Bowen

Mackay

Moranbah

Yeppoon
Rockhampton
Gladstone

Moura

Bundaberg

Maryborough

Fraser I.

Maroochydore

Dalby

Brisbane

Toowoomba

Gold Coast

Goondiwindi

Lismore

Moree

Grafton

Tamworth

Port Macquarie

Narrabri

Dubbo

Maitland

Orange

Newcastle

Bathurst

Gosford

Sydney

Wollongong

Canberra

Cooma

Bega

Eden

Melville I.
Crocker I.
Bathurst I.
*Van Diemen
Gulf*
Wessel Is.

Darwin

*Joseph
Bonaparte
Gulf*

ARNHEM
LAND

Groote Eylandt

Roper

Sir Edward
Pellew Group

Wyndham

Kununurra

Gulf of
Carpentaria

Wellesley Is.

Derby

Durack Range

NORTHERN
TERRITORY

Victoria

Tennant Creek

Mitchell

Gilbert

Norman

Flinders

Leichhardt

Mount Isa

Cloncurry

Charters Towers

Burdekin

Winton

GREAT

G
R
E
A
T

D
I
V
I
D
I
N
G

R
A
N
G
E

GREAT
SANDY
DESERT

AUSTRALIA

QUEENSLAND

Belyando

Alice Springs

Macdonnell Ranges

Georgina

GREAT

ARTESIAN

BASIN

Thomson

Diamantina

Barcoo

Dawson

WESTERN
AUSTRALIA

▲ Ayers Rock

Todd

Musgrave Ranges

GREAT VICTORIA DESERT

Innamincka

Charleville

Roma

Warrego

Oodnadatta

SOUTH
AUSTRALIA

Coober Pedy

*Lake
Eyre
North*

Kalgoorlie-Boulder

NULLARBOR PLAIN

Eucla

Leigh Creek

*Lake
Eyre South*

Flinders Ranges

▲ Mount Painter

Wilcannia

Darling

Barwon

Bourke

Narrabri

NEW

SOUTH WALES

Woomera
*Lake
Gairdner*

*Lake
Torrens*

Broken Hill

Whyalla

▲ Mount Remarkable

Port Pirie

Spencer Gulf

Port Lincoln

Adelaide

Gawler

*Gulf
Saint
Vincent*

Kangaroo I.

Mildura

Balranald

Murrumbidgee

Swan hill

Wagga Wagga

Lachlan

Albury Wadenga

Shepparton

Bendigo

VICTORIA

▲ Mount Kosciuszko

Ballarat

Mount Gambier

Melbourne

Geelong

Warrnambool

Murray

Ovens

King I.

Bass Strait

Flinders I.

Esperance

INDIAN

OCEAN

Tasman

Sea

Burnie

George Town

Launceston

Mount Ossa
▲

Ossa

TASMANIA

Derwent

Hobart

0   500   1000 Miles

0   500   1000   1500 Km

Australia

The Great Dividing Range dominates the eastern highlands. This region of hills and plateaus is not very high—the highest point is Mount Kosciuszko at 7,310 feet—but it separates rivers flowing into the hot interior from those that flow to the Pacific coast. More rain falls on the highlands than on any other part of Australia, and the region's fertile soil supports Australia's most productive farms. Farmers in the states of New South Wales and Victoria grow rice, wheat, barley, vegetables, sugarcane, oranges and other fruits, and grapes for making wine. Others specialize in beef and dairy produce. Farmers farther north, along the coast of the state of Queensland, concentrate on raising sugarcane and tropical fruits such as bananas and grapefruit.

Australia is one of the world's leading exporters of diamonds, lead, and bauxite (the principal ore of aluminum) and is a major supplier of iron ore, nickel, silver, tin, copper, gold, tungsten, and zinc. Australian miners also produce gypsum and asbestos, which are used for making construction materials, and uranium, which powers nuclear plants. Coal, oil, and gas fields provide much of Australia's

energy needs and are supplemented by some of the world's biggest solar energy complexes.

Manufacturing and service industries create more than three-quarters of the country's jobs. Many workers process farm products such as meat, dairy products, wool, sugarcane, and fruit for export. Factories produce furniture, textiles, clothing, shoes, household appliances, and other consumer goods, while heavier industries include iron and steel, car manufacture, chemicals, and paper. Tourism is another important industry. Attractions like the Great Barrier Reef and Ayers Rock provide thousands of jobs and attract more than one million visitors every year.

Because of the country's successful economy, most Australians enjoy a high standard of living, with comfortable housing, well-developed social amenities, and excellent educational and health systems. In addition to supporting sports facilities of nearly every kind, the cities also cater to a wide variety of cultural tastes, with some of the world's finest opera houses, concert halls, theaters, and art galleries. Medical and educational support is also

Above: Downtown office blocks form a backdrop to Sydney's spectacular modern Opera House.

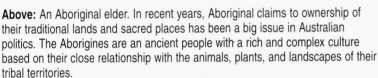

Above: An Aboriginal elder. In recent years, Aboriginal claims to ownership of their traditional lands and sacred places has been a big issue in Australian politics. The Aborigines are an ancient people with a rich and complex culture based on their close relationship with the animals, plants, and landscapes of their tribal territories.

available to the 13 percent of the population who live in the widely scattered mining settlements and sheep stations (ranches) of the interior, commonly called the **outback.** Members of Australia's famous Royal Flying Doctor Service are always ready to go to the outback to give urgent medical assistance. Teachers use two-way radios to reach young people studying at home.

More than 40,000 years ago, Australia's indigenous people, the Aborigines, arrived from Southeast Asia. They traveled by raft or canoe across the shallow seas that separated Asia and Australia at that time. Numbering more than 200,000, they live mainly in rural areas of the states of New South Wales, Queensland, and Northern Territory. In recent decades, many young Aborigines have moved to the towns, but most are disadvantaged in terms of education, employment, and living standards. Many Aborigines feel a great sense of injustice at the treatment of their people, their ancient culture, and their ancestral lands by the overwhelmingly dominant European-descended population.

European settlement began with a British penal colony in New South Wales in 1788. But exploration and voluntary settlement developed rapidly through the nineteenth century, based principally on mining and sheep farming. The fledgling states of Australia joined together under a **federal** constitution in 1901. The British monarch is head of state and is represented in Australia by a governor-general.

Australia still has close links with Britain, but since the 1960s, trade has become more and more focused on Asia, especially Japan and China, and on the United States. Partly as a result of this shift, many Australians believe the time has come for the country to break its historic ties with Britain and to become a republic. Another factor has been the change in Australia's population mixture. Historically, England, Scotland, Ireland, Germany, and the Netherlands supplied most of Australia's immigrants, But the country relaxed its immigration laws in the 1960s, and since then new waves of immigrants have arrived from Greece, Italy, eastern Europe, the Middle East, and Asia.

Above: The main road from the state of Western Australia to the cities of southeastern Australia runs close to the southern coast, across the dry, flat expanse of the Nullarbor Plain. The plain is well named. Nullarbor comes from the Latin words *nullus* and *arbor*—meaning "no tree."

Papua New Guinea

Papua New Guinea

Status:	Constitutional Monarchy
Area:	178,703 square miles
Population:	4.7 million
Capital:	Port Moresby
Languages:	English, Pidgin English, Motu
Currency:	Kina (100 toea)

Papua New Guinea consists of the eastern half of the island of New Guinea and more than 600 smaller islands, including New Britain, the Bismarck **Archipelago,** Bougainville Island, the Louisiade Archipelago, and the D'Entrecasteaux Islands. Papua New Guinea's nearest neighbors are Indonesia, Malaysia, and the Philippines to the west and northwest and Australia to the south. In the late nineteenth century, parts of the region were controlled by Germany and then Britain. After World War I (1914–1918), the island became a mandated territory under the **League of Nations.** By the end of World War II (1939–1945), the **United Nations** (UN, the league's successor) had declared it a **trust territory** to be administered by Australia. Papua New Guinea became independent in 1975 but maintains close ties to Australia.

Mountains that reach 8,000 to 14,000 feet above sea level dominate the interior of the main island. In between the mountains are steep river gorges. **Tropical rain forests** cover most of the land, but broad valleys and basins within the mountains provide large areas of rich soil that support most of the country's agriculture. Most of Papua New Guinea's people live in these highland valleys and basins, where the climate is cooler and healthier than it is on the coast.

Papua New Guinea's hot, humid coastal plains support a number of large towns—Wewak, Madang, Lae, and Popondetta on the north coast and Kerema, Kupiano, and the capital of Port Moresby in the south. However, swamps cover large parts of the coast, and few people live in these areas.

Below: Mount Hagen tribesmen in full ceremonial costume gather for a feast. Shells and wild boar tusks decorate their belts and necklaces, and bird of paradise feathers adorn their magnificent headdresses. A bird of paradise is featured on the country's flag.

Most of Papua New Guinea's people live in small villages, where hundreds of dialects are spoken and where there is a huge variety of traditions and customs. Farmers on most of the islands grow **taro** and bananas in the wetter areas and sweet potatoes, coconuts, and vegetables and fruits on the drier soils. Pigs and chickens provide meat for most families. Farmers on small holdings and on large plantations produce cash crops for export. The principal commercial crops are coffee beans, cacao beans, **copra** (dried coconut meat that can be processed into oil), and tea, with smaller amounts of peanuts, tobacco, rubber, and pyrethrum (used to make insecticides).

The farmers who live in the forested regions of the mountainous interior follow an age-old farming practice called shifting cultivation. According to this practice, farmers clear the land of trees and undergrowth, which are then burned. The resulting ash fertilizes the soil, allowing crops to be grown for two or three years. The farmers move on, clearing a new patch and enabling the forest to regenerate trees and undergrowth in the old plot.

Forestry workers extract hardwoods for export as logs, sawn lumber, plywood, and veneers. These goods are destined mainly for Australia, Asia, and Europe. Fishers catch many species for the home and export markets, the most valuable export being skipjack tuna.

Factories in Port Moresby, Lae, Madang, Bulolo, and Goroka on the main island, in Kieta on Bougainville Island, and in Rabaul on New Britain process farm and forest produce and manufacture furniture, textiles, clothing, cement, and chemicals. Papua New Guinea has many large mineral deposits, but many are in inaccessible regions and so far have not been exploited. Natural gas fields around the Gulf of Papua produce energy for the country. The chief mineral exports are copper and gold. One of the world's biggest copper mines is located at Panguna on Bougainville Island. Japan, Germany, and Spain buy the bulk of the copper exports. Papua New Guinea is not wealthy, but its government is using the profits of its developing economy to improve access to health-care and educational services.

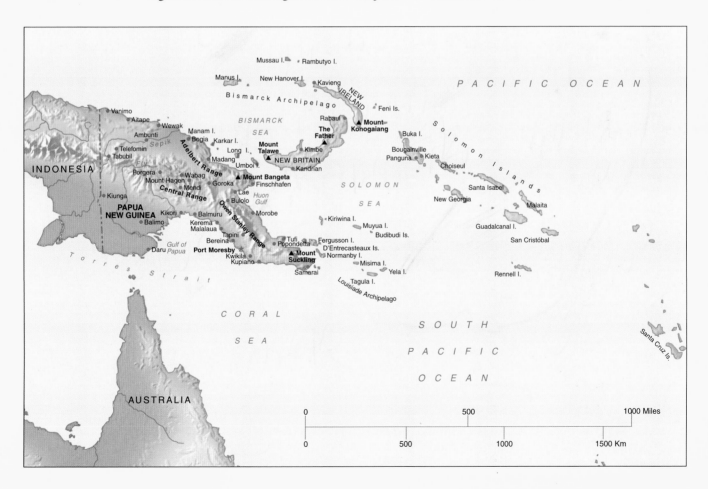

New Zealand

Status:	Constitutional Monarchy
Area:	104,452 square miles
Population:	3.8 million
Capital:	Wellington
Languages:	English, Maori
Currency:	New Zealand dollar (100 cents)

Above: Lush grazing land lies in the eastern part of North Island.

New Zealand, separated from Australia by the Tasman Sea, lies almost 1,000 miles southeast of its giant neighbor. New Zealand's two main islands—North and South—and a scattering of smaller ones form the southernmost islands of Polynesia. Geological activity thrust the islands above sea level recently—at least in geologic time. South Island broke the surface 10 to 15 million years ago, and parts of North Island pushed upward within the past 5 million years.

Volcanic mountains cover the central and western portions of North Island. The tallest peak is Mount Ruapehu, which rises to 9,175 feet above sea level. Thick layers of volcanic soil extend over much of the land, creating fertile farmland. **Geysers** and bubbling mud pools attract millions of tourists and provide New Zealand with a valuable energy source. Holes drilled deep into the ground tap superheated steam, which is used to drive the turbines of **geothermal power** stations. Low hills in eastern North Island offer grazing for beef cattle, dairy herds, and sheep, while farmers in the region's coastal lowlands grow fruits and vegetables. Forests, sandy beaches, and sheltered inlets make the ragged northern peninsula a popular vacation area.

The larger South Island is dominated by the Southern Alps, which angle across the country from northeast to southwest. Snowfields and glaciers cover Mount Cook (12,349 feet) and other neighboring peaks, which tower above forested slopes and beautiful lakes. Stunning mountain scenery attracts hikers and climbers from all over the world. Dense forests cover the western slopes of the Alps, which drop steeply to a narrow coastal plain. To the east, the mountains slope more gently to the broad, flat Canterbury

Plains and to the rolling hills of Otago in the south. The Canterbury Plains provide New Zealand's only extensive lowland area, where farmers grow wheat, barley, oats, and fodder crops.

Cropland and pasture are New Zealand's greatest assets, supporting nearly 60 million sheep and about 8 million cattle. Mutton, lamb, beef, dairy produce, and wool are exported to Australia, Britain, Europe, Japan, and the United States and make up about half the country's export earnings. New Zealand farmers are also the world's principal suppliers of kiwi fruit. A thriving fishing industry hauls in crabs, lobsters, and shellfish for the home market and for export. New Zealand's forestry industry supports lumber, plywood, and paper factories. More than 90 percent of the wood comes from plantations of pine.

Hydroelectric stations on rivers supply about 75 percent of New Zealand's energy needs. Geothermal energy, coal, oil, and natural gas provide the rest. New Zealand's modest reserves of iron ore, gold, silver, and tungsten are insufficient to support heavy industry, so iron and steel, industrial machinery, cars, buses, trucks, and oil are the country's principal imports. Factories concentrated around Dunedin and Christchurch on South Island and around Wellington (the nation's capital) and Auckland on North Island produce textiles, clothing, food products, furniture, metal goods, chemicals, and petroleum products.

New Zealand's mixed economy supports a high standard of living. Most people live in comfortable, well-equipped homes. Excellent health-care and educational services are available to everyone. The cities provide theaters, galleries, and other cultural attractions, and most towns have a wide range of sports facilities. The countryside caters to nearly every outdoor activity from skiing to sailing.

The first settlers in New Zealand were the **Maori,** who arrived from islands elsewhere in Polynesia more than 1,000 years ago. The Maori make up about 15 percent of the population, with the remaining 85 percent being the descendants of British immigrants who began to arrive in the 1800s. Equal opportunity is a hallmark of the New Zealand way of life, and many Maori have achieved prominence in business and public office. The national government is still trying to resolve long-standing disputes over land rights. It is also attempting to improve educational and job opportunities for low-income Maori.

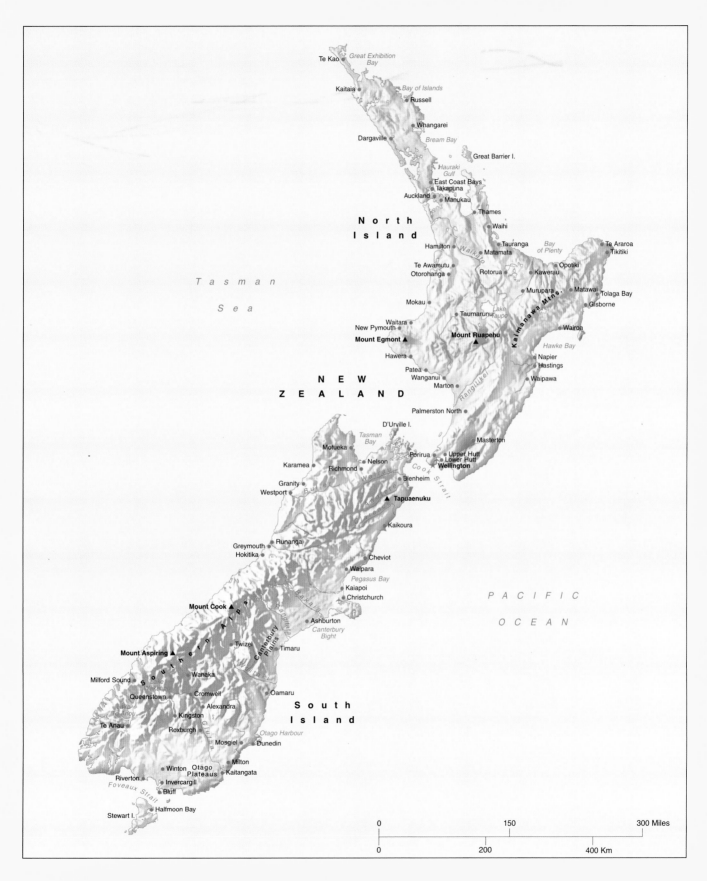

Te Kao

Great Exhibition Bay

Kaitaia

Bay of Islands

Russell

Whangarei

Dargaville

Bream Bay

Great Barrier I.

Hauraki Gulf

East Coast Bays
Takapuna

Auckland
Manukau

Thames

Waihi

North Island

Hamilton

Waikato

Tauranga

Bay of Plenty

Te Araroa
Tikitiki

Matamata

Te Awamutu

Rotorua

Kawerau

Opotiki

Otorohanga

Murupara

Matawai

Tolaga Bay

T a s m a n

S e a

Mokau

Kaimanawa Mtns.

Gisborne

Taumarunui

Lake Taupo

Waitara

Wairoa

New Pymouth

Mount Egmont ▲

Mount Ruapehu ▲

Rangitikei

Hawke Bay

Hawera

Napier

Patea

Hastings

N E W

Wanganui

Waipawa

Marton

Z E A L A N D

Palmerston North

D'Urville I.

Masterton

Tasman Bay

Motueka

Upper Hutt
Lower Hutt

Porirua

Wellington

Karamea

Richmond

Nelson

Cook Strait

Granity

Buller

Blenheim

Westport

▲ **Tapuaenuku**

Kaikoura

Greymouth

Runanga

Hokitika

Cheviot

Waipara

Pegasus Bay

Kaiapoi

P A C I F I C

Christchurch

O C E A N

Mount Cook ▲

S o u t h e r n   A l p s

Ashburton

Canterbury Bight

Twizel

Canterbury Plains

Mount Aspiring ▲

Timaru

Milford Sound

Wanaka

Queenstown

Cromwell

Oamaru

Alexandra

South Island

Kingston

Te Anau

Roxburgh

Otago Harbour

Mosgiel

Dunedin

Milton

Winton

Otago Plateaus

Kaitangata

Riverton

Invercargill

Bluff

Foveaux Strait

Stewart I.

Halfmoon Bay

0		150		300 Miles

0	200		400 Km

15

Northern Marianas and Guam

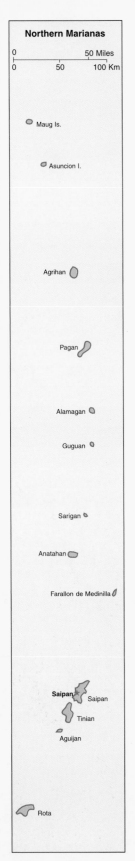

Northern Marianas

0   50 Miles
0   50   100 Km

Maug Is.

Asuncion I.

Agrihan

Pagan

Alamagan

Guguan

Sarigan

Anatahan

Farallon de Medinilla

Saipan   Saipan

Tinian

Aguijan

Rota

Northern Marianas

Status:	Self-governing Commonwealth of the United States
Area:	184 square miles
Population:	47,000
Capital:	Saipan
Languages:	English, Chamorro
Currency:	U.S. dollar (100 cents)

Self-governing since 1978, the territory of the Northern Marianas includes all the Marianas Islands except Guam. The islands make up the northernmost group of islands in Micronesia.

The islands are actually the tops of submarine volcanoes strung out in a chain across the northern Pacific Ocean. The highest, most rugged, and youngest islands are at the northern end of the chain and still experience volcanic eruptions. Pagan, Agrihan, and Anatahan are the three largest islands in this group. The southern islands in the Marianas are older. Erosion has worn down their volcanic peaks, and **coral reefs** have grown up around their shores. Saipan, Tinian, and Rota are the largest in this group.

Native islanders—who are called the Chamorro—are descended from settlers who came to the islands from the Asian mainland thousands of years ago. Since then, Europeans, Filipinos, and others have joined the population. The commonwealth status of the Marianas confers U.S. citizenship on the people who live there. Fishing and farming provide some of the food required, but additional supplies are imported from the United States. Tourism is the principal economic activity.

Below: Dramatic cliffs line parts of the coast of Saipan Island in the Northern Marianas.

Guam

Status:	External Territory of the United States
Area:	212 square miles
Population:	200,000
Capital:	Agana
Languages:	Chamorro, English
Currency:	U.S. dollar (100 cents)

Guam is the largest and southernmost island in the Marianas group. Its original inhabitants arrived from Asia more than 2,000 years ago and perhaps as long ago as 3000 B.C. The island's modern population includes people whose ancestors immigrated from the Philippines, Japan, China, Indonesia, the United States, and Europe.

Densely forested volcanic mountains dominate the south of the island, while the north consists of a limestone plateau edged by coastal plains. Workers cleared most of the forests that once covered the north and west of the island to make way for the large U.S. naval and air force facilities that provide jobs for many of the local people.

White sandy beaches fringe most of the coast, with coral reefs offshore. These natural attractions support tourism, another major source of income. Thousands of tourists, mainly from Japan, visit Guam each year. Local farmers grow sweet potatoes, taro, coconuts, and fruits, and fishers catch tuna and other fish in the surrounding waters. But most of the island's food supplies are imported from the United States. Small businesses on Guam make textiles and process tobacco and copra for export.

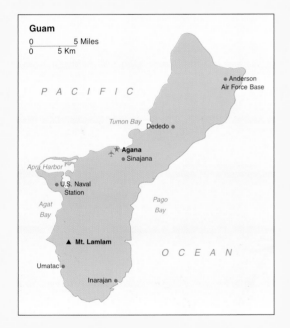

Right: A nineteenth-century lookout post guards one of Guam's many bays. The War in the Pacific National Historical Park on Guam commemorates U.S. troops who fought in World War II.

Federated States of Micronesia and Palau

Federated States of Micronesia

Status:	Republic
Area:	270 square miles
Population:	100,000
Capital:	Palikir
Languages:	English, local languages
Currency:	U.S. dollar (100 cents)

The Federated States of Micronesia consist of more than 600 islands and tiny coral islets in the Caroline Islands archipelago. Scattered across 1,500 miles of the North Pacific Ocean, the islands are clustered into four groups, which are also administrative units, or states—Yap, Chuuk, Pohnpei, and Kosrae. Each of the states has a dominant local language that is used alongside English, the official language. More than one-fourth of Micronesia's people live in the capital, Palikir, on the main island of Pohnpei. After wartime occupation by the Japanese, the islands were a UN trust territory from 1947 to 1986, when they gained full independence. The United States ensures the islands' defense under a special agreement.

Tropical rain forests cover much of the land of the larger, higher islands, with mangrove forests fringing the coasts. The thin, sandy soil of the smaller coral islands cannot support such dense vegetation, so their main vegetation consists of sparse grasses and stands of coconut trees, breadfruit trees, and pandanus palms. Most of the people live in small village communities and make their living from subsistence farming and fishing. Farmers raise breadfruit, taro, bananas, and coconuts for food and prepare copra for export. The copra is processed abroad to yield coconut oil. Micronesia's fishers catch a variety of fish and shellfish for local use. The islands also receive payments from U.S., Japanese, and Korean fishing fleets in return for permission to catch tuna in the islands' territorial waters. Miners extract small amounts of phosphate, which is exported to make fertilizer. These sources of income, however, do not earn enough to pay for all the goods Micronesia needs to import, and the islands' economy depends heavily on grants from the United States.

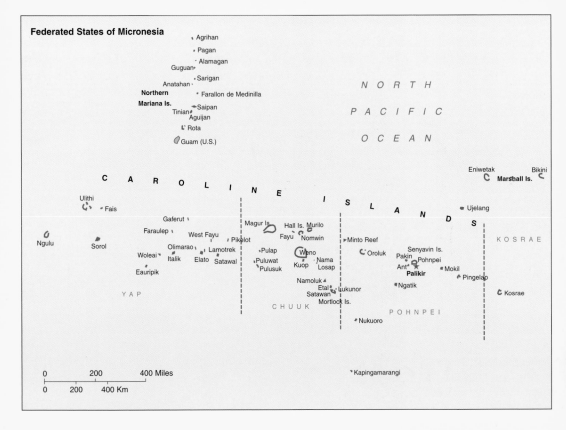

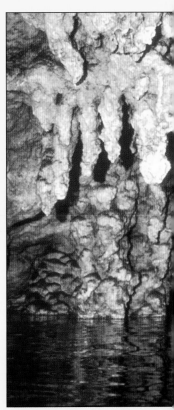

Palau

Babelthuap

Koror Koror

P h i l i p p i n e

S e a

Nigeruktabel

Eli Malk

Beliliou

Angaurou

N O R T H

P A C I F I C

O C E A N

Helen I.

Kayangel Is.

| 0 | 25 | 50 | 75 Miles |
| 0 | 25 | 50 | 75 Km |

Palau

Status:	Republic
Area:	178 square miles
Population:	17,000
Capital:	Koror
Languages:	Palauan, English
Currency:	U.S. dollar (100 cents)

Palau consists of a cluster of more than 200 islands and small coral islets. The group sits to the west of the Caroline Islands. Most of Palau's inhabitants live on the small island of Koror, which lies in the middle of the group. The rest of the population is spread over seven other nearby islands. The present capital, built on Koror and sharing the same name, grew up around the island's fine deepwater harbor. But the city has no room to expand, and a new administrative center is being built on the much larger island of Babelthuap to the north, where broad coastal plains surround a mountainous interior.

Palau gained independence in 1994—the last of the U.S. administered Pacific trust territories to do so. Like Micronesia, Palau has a special agreement under which the United States is responsible for the islands' security and defense.

Most of the people of Palau are subsistence farmers or fishers. Many others are employed by the government or in the islands' growing tourist industry. Farmers grow taro, cassava, sweet potatoes, coconuts, and other fruits and vegetables. They export copra as their main cash crop. Fishers concentrate chiefly on high-value tuna for export. Scuba diving, snorkeling, sailing, and sport fishing attract large numbers of visitors each year, principally from the United States, Japan, Taiwan, and Hong Kong.

Left: These spectacular limestone caverns are at Babelthuap on Palau.

19

Marshall Islands and Nauru

Marshall Islands

Status:	Republic in Free Association with the United States
Area:	69 square miles
Population:	100,000
Capital:	Majuro
Languages:	English, Marshallese dialects
Currency:	U.S. dollar (100 cents)

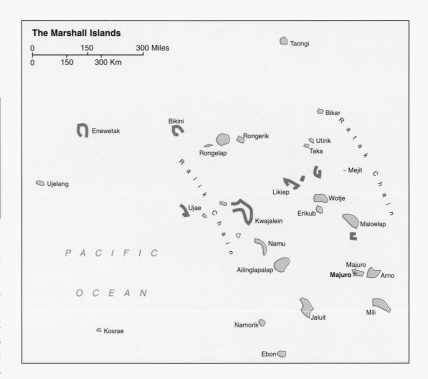

The Marshall Islands

The Marshall Islands total more than 1,000 coral islands, tiny islets, **atolls,** and reefs in eastern Micronesia. The islands form two parallel chains that are 125 miles apart and about 620 miles long. The eastern chain is called the Ratak (Sunrise) Chain. The western one is the Ralik (Sunset) Chain. American military scientists carried out nuclear tests on two of the northernmost islands—Enewetak and Bikini—between 1946 and 1958. Radioactive contamination has meant those islands have remained uninhabited since that time. The United States still maintains a large military base on Kwajalein Atoll.

The fine coral sand that covers the islands is unsuited to agriculture, but local farmers manage to grow the few crops—coconut palms, banana papayas, and breadfruit trees—that can tolerate the conditions. Copra, from which coconut oil is extracted, is the main agricultural export. But the economy depends largely on tourism and on money paid by the United States for its use of the islands as military bases.

Below: Many of the tourists who visit the Marshall Islands go diving on the coral reefs, which have an abundant array of tropical fish and sea life.

Nauru

Status:	Republic
Area:	8 square miles
Population:	11,000
Capital:	Yaren (unofficial)
Languages:	Nauruan, English
Currency:	Australian dollar (100 cents)

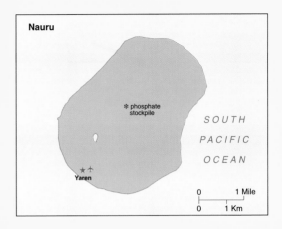

Nauru

※ phosphate stockpile

SOUTH PACIFIC OCEAN

Yaren

0   1 Mile
0   1 Km

Nauru, a tiny speck of land in the west central Pacific Ocean just south of the equator, is the third-smallest country in the world. Only Vatican City and Monaco are smaller in land area. The country consists of a single oval coral island that is three miles wide and three-and-a-half miles long. A narrow fertile coastal plain encircles a dry central plateau that rises to 225 feet above sea level. Most Nauruans live in small settlements that dot the coast. There is no official capital, but the largest settlement, Yaren, on the southern coast, serves as the country's administrative center.

Native islanders of Polynesian, Micronesian, and Melanesian descent make up about two-thirds of Nauru's population. The remaining one-third are nearly all contract workers from neighboring Pacific islands, from Hong Kong in China, and from Australia. These workers labor in the island's phosphate-mining industry.

High-grade phosphate rock is Nauru's sole valuable natural resource and is exported all around the Pacific as a raw material for making fertilizer. For the past 30 years, income from phosphate exports has provided the islanders with a high standard of living, free schools, free medical services, and government-subsidized housing. But there has been a high price to pay. Mining has left the island's interior a desolate wasteland of bare rock and spoil heaps, and the phosphate reserves are almost exhausted. Britain and Australia—partners in the exploitation of the phosphates—have paid large sums in compensation, but the Nauruan government is looking for new sources of income and employment. Options include expanding the country's fishing industry, promoting tourism, expanding the airport at Yaren as a hub for Pacific air traffic, and developing the island's financial services as a tax haven for businesses and wealthy individuals.

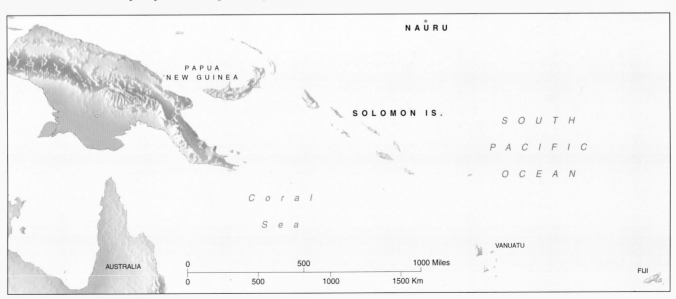

NAURU

PAPUA NEW GUINEA

SOLOMON IS.

SOUTH PACIFIC OCEAN

Coral Sea

VANUATU

AUSTRALIA

0   500   1000 Miles
0   500   1000   1500 Km

FIJI

Solomon Islands and Vanuatu

Solomon Islands

Status:	Constitutional Monarchy
Area:	11,158 square miles
Population:	400,000
Capital:	Honiara
Language:	English
Currency:	Solomon Islands dollar (100 cents)

The Solomon Islands are located in the southwestern Pacific Ocean, about 1,000 miles northeast of Australia. Six main islands account for most of the country's land area—Choiseul, Santa Isabel, New Georgia, Guadalcanal, Malaita, and San Cristobal. The Solomons also include many smaller islands. Guadalcanal is the largest island and contains the capital, Honiara, home to about 10 percent of the population. Britain ruled the Solomon Islands as a **protectorate** from 1893 until the country became fully independent in 1978 as a member of the **British Commonwealth.**

Steep, rugged, densely forested volcanic mountains dominate the interior of the principal islands, rising to about 4,000 feet in places. Narrow coastal plains fringe the shores, providing fertile soils for the country's farmers. Climate varies from year-round heat and humidity in the north to a milder, more seasonal climate in the south.

Almost 90 percent of the islanders make their living from farming. They grow a variety of fruits and vegetables as food crops and raise cacao beans, palms (for oil), and coconut trees (for copra) as export crops. Fishing—especially for tuna—and timber from the rich hardwood forests provide the biggest share of the islands' export earnings. Miners on Bellona Island, south of the main group, produce phosphates for export.

Japan is the country's biggest customer for all these commodities. Exports are essential to the islands, because most manufactured goods and energy supplies have to be imported. The country has few industries. The difficult terrain, which makes road building almost impossible, restricts development.

Below: Children enjoy a traditional game on Malaita Island in the Solomon Islands. Their tightly curled hair is a characteristic of the Melanesian people.

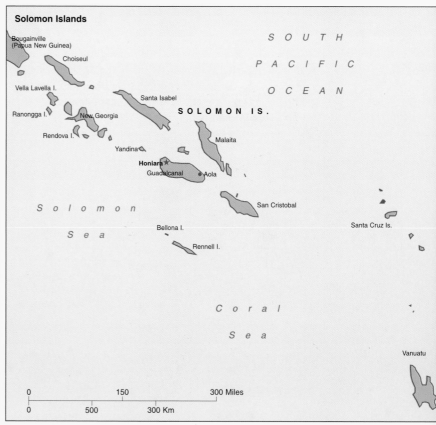

Vanuatu

Status:	Republic
Area:	4,707 square miles
Population:	200,000
Capital:	Port-Vila
Languages:	Bislama, English, French
Currency:	Vatu (100 centimes)

Thirteen large islands and 70 smaller ones make up the territory of Vanuatu in the southwestern Pacific. Britain and France governed the islands, then known as the New Hebrides, from 1906 to 1980, when Vanuatu became an independent country.

Volcanic eruptions on the Pacific seabed created the Y-shaped island chain of Vanuatu, and several of the islands still have active volcanoes. Because the islands are geologically young, their interiors are still rugged and mountainous, with forested hills sloping steeply down to narrow coastal plains where fertile soil supports farming. Most of the people live in small villages in houses made of bamboo and thatched with palm fronds. The farmers grow a variety of fruits and vegetables and raise chickens, cattle, and pigs. Much of the food is used locally, although many farmers also produce copra and cacao beans as cash crops for export. Like many island nations, Vanuatu has a tradition of fishing, and fish and shellfish are an important part of the diet. The capital of Port-Vila on Éfaté Island and the city of Santo on Espiritu Santo are the only urban centers of any size.

With no industry, no mineral resources, and terrain that makes road building extremely difficult, Vanuatu makes full use of its internal air transport system and its coastal freight and passenger boats. Tourism is the fastest-growing industry and an important provider of jobs. The islands' hot climate, spectacular mountain scenery, exotic flowers and birds, and extensive reefs attract large numbers of visitors, principally from Japan and Australia.

Above: An outdoor food market at Port-Vila, Vanuatu

Fiji and New Caledonia

Fiji

Status:	Republic
Area:	7,054 square miles
Population:	800,000
Capital:	Suva
Languages:	Fijian, Hindi, English
Currency:	Fijian dollar (100 cents)

With 800,000 people inhabiting about 100 of the country's more than 300 islands, Fiji has the largest population of any of the Pacific island countries with the exception of Papua New Guinea. Two ethnic groups dominate life in Fiji. Native Fijians—Melanesians who have populated the islands for thousands of years—make up 46 percent of the population. The Fijians own most of the land and control the government and administration. Another 49 percent consists of Indians who are the descendants of workers brought in by the British in the 1800s. The Indian community dominates the professional and business life of the islands. Fijians fear losing control, and Indians resent being treated as second-class citizens. These conflicting interests have troubled the islands since Fiji ceased to be a British **colony** and became independent in 1970.

Fiji's two largest islands, Vanua Levu and Viti Levu, account for most of the country's land area. Volcanic eruptions created the islands, and their interiors are still mountainous, rising to 4,341 feet at Mount Tomanivi on Viti Levu. About 30 other peaks exceed 3,000 feet above sea level. Coral reefs ring the main islands. The smaller islands consist almost entirely of coral.

Fertile volcanic soils on the coastal lowlands of the main islands support most of Fiji's agriculture. Fijian farmers grow rice, fruits, and vegetables for local use, and many also raise pigs and chickens. Processed sugar is Fiji's principal export, and Indian tenant farmers grow most of the sugarcane on small holdings leased from Fijian landowners. Factory workers in large sugar mills at Lautoka, Labasa, and Bua process the cane into sugar. Coconuts are the second most valuable

Above: Mountain peaks rise dramatically in the northwest of Viti Levu, Fiji.

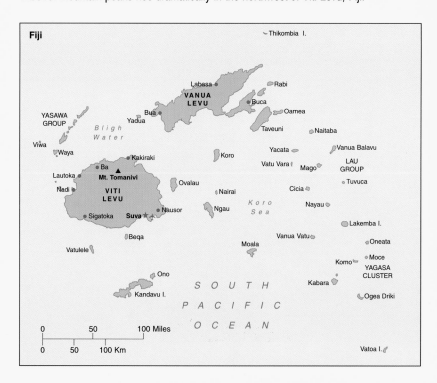

crop. The copra is transported to factories in the capital city of Suva, where it is pressed to produce coconut oil for export. In recent years, Fiji's farmers have started growing cacao beans and ginger to broaden the range of agricultural exports. Fiji's main customers are Britain, Europe, Malaysia, China, Australia, New Zealand, and the United States.

Miners on Viti Levu extract gold for export, and manufacturing plants in the main towns produce textiles, clothing, furniture, farm machinery, and other goods, mainly for local use. Fiji's beautiful beaches and scenery, pleasant climate, clear waters, and countless reefs support a thriving tourist industry that provides many jobs in hotels, in restaurants, in transportation, and in other services.

Left: A Melanesian resident from the Isle of Pines

New Caledonia

Status:	Overseas Territory of France
Area:	7,174 square miles
Population:	200,000
Capital:	Nouméa
Languages:	French, Melanesian and Polynesian dialects
Currency:	CFP franc (100 centimes)

New Caledonia, an overseas territory of France, is one of the most southwesterly of the Melanesian islands and lies about 820 miles northeast of Brisbane, Australia. The main island is 250 miles long and 30 miles wide and is completely ringed by coral reefs. The Loyalty Islands, the Isle of Pines, and the Bélép Islands are dependencies of New Caledonia.

Native Melanesians make up 43 percent of the population, Europeans account for 37 percent, with Polynesians and Indonesians making up most of the remainder. One commodity—nickel—dominates New Caledonia's economy. The country is one of the world's leading suppliers. Miners extract the ore from large open-pit mines at Poro and Thio on New Caledonia's northern coast and at Nepoui on the southern coast. The ore is

purified for export at a huge smelting plant at Doniambo, near the capital.

Tourism is New Caledonia's second-biggest source of income. The islands lie about 1,500 miles south of the equator and have a pleasant climate with well-marked seasons. Clear waters and extensive reefs attract divers and snorkelers, while the scenery, beaches, and old colonial architecture draw visitors from many parts of the world. Unfortunately, political unrest has damaged the tourist industry in recent years, but the islands' natural resources—combined with financial support from France—still ensure good living standards, educational opportunities, and health-care services for New Caledonia's people.

Tuvalu and Wallis and Futuna Islands

Tuvalu

Status:	Parliamentary Monarchy
Area:	10 square miles
Population:	10,000
Capital:	Funafuti
Languages:	Tuvaluan, English
Currency:	Australian dollar (100 cents)

The nine coral islands that make up Tuvalu have a total land area that ranks them as the fourth-smallest country in the world, after Vatican City, Monaco, and Nauru. Nowhere does the land rise more than 15 feet above sea level. Almost one-third of the Tuvaluan people live on Funafuti Atoll, home of the national capital (also called Funafuti) and the country's airport.

Most Tuvaluan people live in small communities and make their living by farming and fishing. The islands' poor soil consists almost entirely of coral sand and is unsuitable for most plants. Farmers rely on species like coconut palms, pandanus palms, bananas, and taro that can tolerate the harsh conditions. Most islanders also raise pigs and chickens for food. Copra is the only significant farm export. Fish are an important part of the local diet and are also a source of income—both from selling fish and from selling fishing licenses to boat operators from Japan and the United States. Apart from artisans making mats, baskets, and carvings, there is no manufacturing, and many Tuvaluans seek jobs abroad or on cruise ships. Britain, Australia, New Zealand, and Japan help to support the Tuvaluan economy with financial grants.

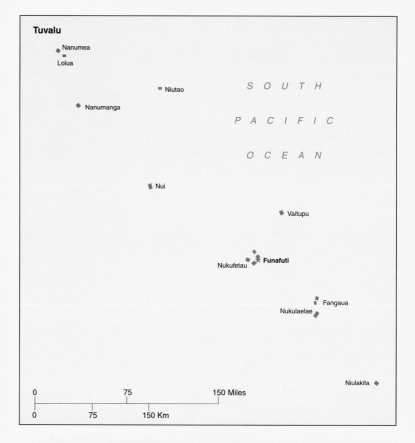

Right: A coconut grove on Tuvalu. The farming of coconuts for the production of copra is an important part of the Tuvaluan economy.

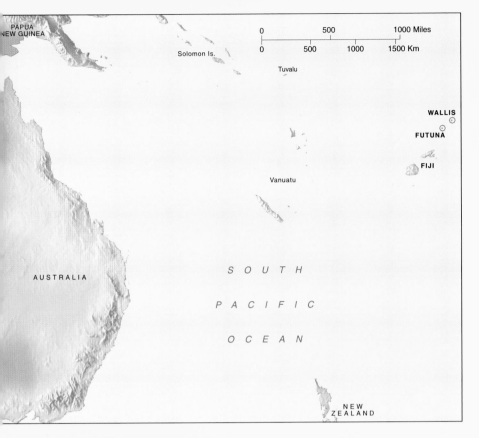

Wallis and Futuna Islands

Status:	Self-governing Overseas Territory of France
Area:	77 square miles
Population:	14,000
Capital:	Mata-Utu
Languages:	French, Wallisian, Futunian
Currency:	CFP franc (100 centimes)

The Wallis and Futuna Islands lie about 300 miles northeast of Fiji and consist of three main islands—Futuna, Alofi, and Uvea—plus a scattering of smaller islands, reefs, and atolls. Uvea, the principal island of the Wallis group, is by far the largest and is home to about 60 percent of the country's people. It also contains the largest settlement—the capital Mata-Utu, with a population of about 850. Hills cover the interior of the island, with low plains around the coast and coral reefs offshore. Futuna and Alofi are higher, with more rugged, mountainous interiors and narrower coastal plains.

The islands have no natural resources, and most of the islanders make their living by subsistence farming and fishing. Most grow **cassava,** sweet potatoes, and bananas as their main food crops and coconut trees as a source of copra, which is sold for processing to yield coconut oil. The economy of the islands depends greatly on financial aid from France.

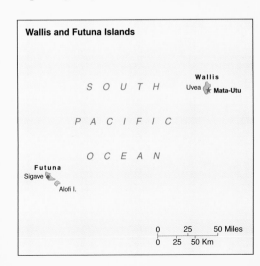

Western Samoa, American Samoa, Tonga

Western Samoa

Status:	Constitutional Monarchy
Area:	1,097 square miles
Population:	200,000
Capital:	Apia
Languages:	Samoan, English
Currency:	Tala (100 sene)

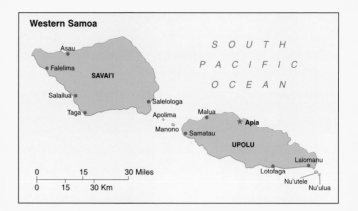

Western Samoa's people inhabit two large islands, Savai'i and Upolu, and two smaller islands, Apolima and Manono, which lie in the Apolima Strait between the main islands. Five other islands are uninhabited. Two-thirds of the Samoan people live on Upolu, the smaller, lower, and more fertile of the main islands. Volcanic mountains dominate the interior of Savai'i and Upolu, dropping steeply to narrow fertile plains around the coasts. Dense tropical rain forests cover the interior regions.

Most of the people live in village communities and make their living by farming and fishing. The climate is warm and tropical, and typical Samoan houses have thick thatched roofs to provide shade and open sides to let in cool breezes. In wet, windy weather, the owners let down woven palm-leaf curtains to keep their homes warm and dry. Samoan farmers grow bananas, breadfruit, taro, and other fruits and vegetables for their own use. Many also keep pigs and chickens. Coconuts (for producing copra), taro, and cacao beans are the principal commercial crops. New Zealand buys most of Western Samoa's farm exports.

Western Samoa is not a rich country, but its people enjoy a good standard of living. The government, small businesses, and a thriving tourist industry provide employment. The government also supplies free health-care services and free schooling.

Above: An agile youngster climbs for coconuts in Western Samoa.

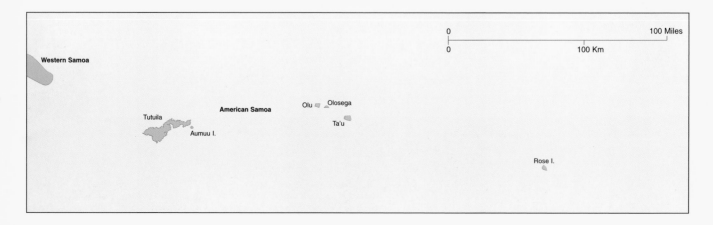

American Samoa

Status:	Self-governing Territory of the United States
Area:	77 square miles
Population:	56,000
Capital:	Pago Pago
Language:	English
Currency:	U.S. dollar (100 cents)

Six of American Samoa's seven islands are part of the island chain that also includes Western Samoa. The seventh island, Swains Island, lies 200 miles away to the north. American Samoa's capital and only large town, Pago Pago, is located on the largest island of Tutuila and is built around one of the finest natural harbors in the Pacific.

Densely forested mountains cover much of the land, with fertile soils in some of the valleys and on the flat coastal plains. Farmers grow taro, coconuts, bananas, and other fruits and vegetables, chiefly for local use. Fishing is one of the principal employers. Tuna meat accounts for more than 95 percent of the country's exports. Some is exported fresh, but most of it is canned in local factories. Virtually the entire catch goes to the United States. The government, tourism, and small factories provide employment for those not engaged in farming and fishing.

With hardly any natural resources, American Samoa would be a poor country were it not for huge financial support from the U.S. government, which pays for health care, schools, and other social services. American Samoa is a self-governing U.S. territory. Its people have right of entry to the United States, and more American Samoans live in Hawaii and the mainland United States than live on the islands. The money they send back to their families provides further help to the local economy.

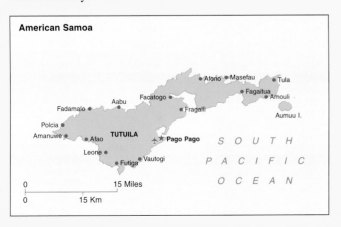

American Samoa

Tonga

Status:	Constitutional Monarchy
Area:	288 square miles
Population:	98,000
Capital:	Nuku'alofa
Languages:	Tongan, English
Currency:	Pa'anga (100 seniti)

In 1773, when the explorer Captain James Cook visited Tonga, the islands' monarchy was already hundreds of years old. The king still has a great deal of power, although there are moves toward greater democracy. Britain governed the country as a protectorate from 1900 until 1970, when Tonga became an independent state and a member of the British Commonwealth.

Tonga's territory covers more than 170 islands that are clustered in three main groups—Ha'apai, Tongatapu, and Vava'u. Almost two-thirds of the people live on Tongatapu, the largest island, where the capital, Nuku'alofa, is located. People inhabit 36 of Tonga's islands. The rest are little more than coral reefs with a few coconut palms and grasses growing in the infertile sand. Volcanic soils on the larger islands support Tonga's agricultural economy. The government owns all the land, but all males age 16 or older are entitled to rent a plot. Three-quarters of all workers make their living in this way. The farmers grow breadfruit, sweet potatoes, cassava, and peanuts. Fishing provides the main protein in the diet. Bananas, copra, coconut oil, and vegetables are the principal exports. Meat, flour, fuel, and manufactured goods are the chief imports. New Zealand and Australia are Tonga's principal trading partners. Tonga's warm, sunny climate, beautiful coast, and stunning mountain scenery attract thousands of tourists every year.

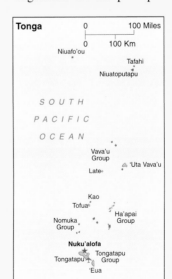

Tonga

Kiribati, Cook Islands, Niue

Kiribati

Status:	Republic
Area:	280 square miles
Population:	79,000
Capital:	Tarawa
Languages:	Kiribati, English
Currency:	Australian dollar (100 cents)

Kiribati is the most widely spread island nation on earth. Its 33 islands are strung out across almost two million square miles of the central and western Pacific Ocean. Kiribati straddles both the equator and the international date line. Its territory consists of the volcanic island of Banaba (formerly called Ocean Island) and three groups of coral islands and atolls—the sixteen islands of the Gilbert Islands group, the eight Phoenix Islands, and eight of the Line Islands. One island—Kiritimati (Christmas Island)—accounts for almost half the nation's total land area. The highest point above sea level on Banaba is a mere 265 feet. Many of Kiribati's smaller islands and atolls stand only 10 to 15 feet above sea level and are at risk of disappearing forever if **global warming** results in a significant rise in world sea levels.

Kiribati was formerly part of the British protectorate of the Gilbert and Ellice Islands. The Ellice Islands separated in 1975 and became the independent nation of Tuvalu in 1978. In 1979 the Gilbert Islands achieved independence as Kiribati.

Mines on Banaba once produced phosphate, but the reserves ran out in 1980, causing severe economic problems. The islanders mainly work in agriculture and fishing and receive foreign aid to supplement their incomes. Most of the people live in small villages, where houses are made of wood with thatched palm roofs. They grow bananas, papayas, breadfruit, sweet potatoes, and taro as their main food crops. Many also raise coconuts to produce copra, which is the principal agricultural export. Fish exports, especially of tuna, account for one-third of the country's income. More money comes from selling fishing licenses to U.S., Japanese, Taiwanese, and Korean fleets.

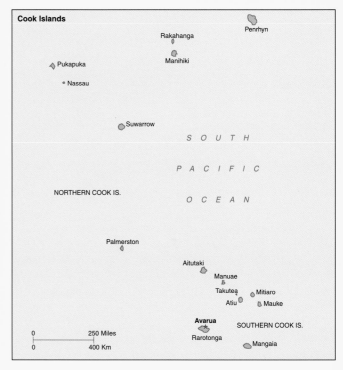

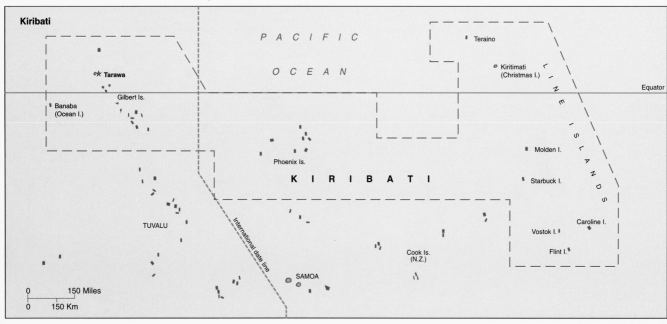

Cook Islands

Status:	Self-governing state in free association with New Zealand
Area:	91 square miles
Population:	19,000
Capital:	Avarua
Language:	English
Currency:	New Zealand dollar (100 cents)

The 15 Cook Islands are spread across roughly 800,000 square miles of the southern Pacific Ocean and are grouped into two clusters—seven in the Northern Cook Islands and eight in the Southern Cook Islands. The northern islands are low coral atolls. Volcanic eruptions formed the much higher and more fertile southern group. The islands are named for Captain James Cook, who, in 1773, was the first European to land on them. Britain passed administrative control of the islands to New Zealand in 1891, and the islands became self-governing in 1965. Under the free association arrangement, the Cook Islanders are New Zealand citizens, and New Zealand is responsible for the islands' defense. Avarua, on Rarotonga Island, is the only large town and serves as the administrative and business center.

Most Cook Islanders live by farming. Bananas, coconuts, pineapples, oranges, and limes are the principal export crops. Factory workers on Rarotonga process and can tropical fruits for export to New Zealand. Other islanders work in small factories producing clothing and crafts. Crews venture off the islands to fish commercially and catch shellfish closer to the coasts.

Below: Cook Islanders use traditional outrigger canoes alongside modern motorboats.

Niue

Status:	Self-governing state in free association with New Zealand
Area:	100 square miles
Population:	2,300
Capital:	Alofi
Language:	English
Currency:	New Zealand dollar (100 cents)

Just 13 miles long and 11 miles wide, the coral island of Niue is a tiny speck in the southern Pacific Ocean between Tonga and the Southern Cook Islands. The people are Polynesian, and their language is closely related to that of Tonga. Although geographically part of the Cook Islands, Niue has been administered separately since 1904 and became independent, in free association with New Zealand, in 1974.

Niue's farmers grow vegetables, coconuts, bananas, passion fruit, and limes. Most of them also raise pigs and chickens. Copra and tropical fruits are the island's principal exports, along with the beautiful baskets and mats the islanders weave from the leaves of the pandanus palm. Fishing, as on most Pacific islands, provides the local people with an important part of their diet. A small, forested region in the middle of the island supplies timber to a sawmill. The island has no other industry, and the economy depends heavily on financial assistance from New Zealand.

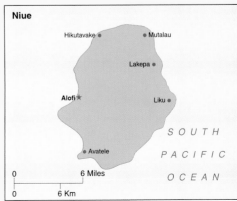

Niue

Hikutavake • • Mutalau

Lakepa •

Alofi ☆ Liku •

• Avatele

SOUTH

PACIFIC

OCEAN

0   6 Miles

0   6 Km

French Polynesia and Pitcairn Island

French Polynesia

Status:	Overseas Territory of France
Area:	1,544 square miles
Population:	200,000
Capital:	Papeete
Languages:	French, Tahitian
Currency:	CFP franc (100 centimes)

French Polynesia comprises 130 islands scattered in five groups across a vast area of the South Pacific Ocean, halfway between Australia and South America. The five groups are the Society Islands, the Marquesas, the Tubuai (Austral) Islands, the Gambier Islands, and the Tuamotu Archipelago. Tahiti, in the Society Islands, is by far the largest of the islands. More than 60 percent of French Polynesia's people live on Tahiti—about 37,000 of them in Papeete, the largest town and the capital of the territory.

The islands of the Tuamotu Archipelago are low coral atolls rising only a few feet above sea level. Their thin, dry, sandy soils are difficult to cultivate, so farmers concentrate on growing coconuts, which are naturally adapted to those conditions. The phosphate mines on Makatea were exhausted in the late 1960s, but pearl diving and collecting mother-of-pearl shells remain important activities.

Volcanic eruptions on the floor of the Pacific Ocean created the other island groups. Rugged mountains fill their interiors, where the steep hills are covered in dense tropical rain forests. Deep river gorges separate the hills from one another. Fertile plains ring the coasts, and most of the islands are encircled by coral reefs enclosing shallow lagoons. Farmers grow sweet potatoes, breadfruit, and taro as their principal food crops. Chickens, pigs, and fish provide meat. Copra, coffee beans, vanilla, peppers, and sugarcane are the main cash crops grown for export, principally to France. The islands' beauty supports a thriving tourist industry that provides jobs in hotels, transportation, sport fishing, and other activities. Trade, tourism, and aid from the French government ensure a high standard of living.

Right: Tourists watch as Polynesian men lift a feast of meat and vegetables from a roasting pit. The food was cooked over hot embers and sealed with palm leaves.

French Polynesia

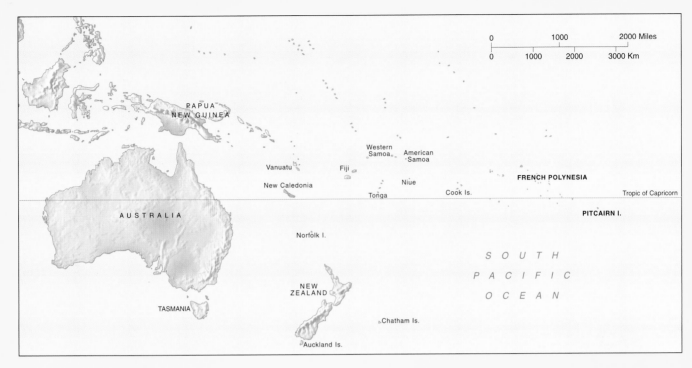

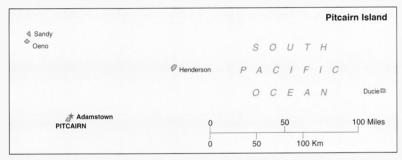

Pitcairn Island

⊲ Sandy
◇ Oeno

◊ Henderson

Ducie ▢

★ Adamstown
PITCAIRN

| 0 | | 50 | | 100 Miles |
| 0 | 50 | | 100 Km | |

Left: Coconut palms shade the clear shallow waters of a reef-ringed lagoon on Motu Island in French Polynesia.

Pitcairn Island

Status:	United Kingdom Dependency
Area:	212 square miles
Population:	70
Capital:	Adamstown
Language:	English
Currency:	New Zealand dollar (100 cents)

Pitcairn Island is famous mainly as the final destination of the mutineers from Captain Bligh's HMS *Bounty,* but it is also one of Britain's most remote dependent territories. This rocky island and its uninhabited neighbors—Henderson, Ducie, and Oeno Islands—lie in the southeastern Pacific, 5,000 miles east of Australia and just south of the **Tropic of Capricorn.**

The island rises steeply from the sea. The land's sheer cliffs lead to high inland areas, where the soil is fertile and the climate is mild and damp. The islanders, mostly descendants of the mutineers and the Polynesian wives they took with them, grow bananas, coconuts, taro, sweet potatoes, and pumpkins.

Antarctica

Antarctica

Status:	Protected International Territory
Area:	5.4 million square miles

Antarctica is a land of extremes. It is the highest, coldest, windiest place on earth. Although covered by water in the form of ice, Antarctica is a desert without a single tree in all its 5.4 million square miles. Seasonal birds such as penguins live on the continent when they breed and hatch their young.

The fifth-largest continent, Antarctica is almost one-and-a-half times the size of the United States. But it has no native people, no flag, no government, no farming, and no industry. Seven countries—Argentina, Australia, Chile, France, Britain, New Zealand, and Norway—have claimed sectors of Antarctica. These claims fan out in pie-shaped slices from the South Pole to the coast and beyond. In 1961, all these countries set aside their territorial claims under the Antarctic Treaty, which preserves the continent for science alone and bans any form of military use, commercial exploitation, or environmental damage. Antarctica has no fixed population, but several thousand scientists and support personnel live there in the summer months. In winter this number dwindles to less than one thousand, who carry out long-term research on climate studies.

Ice, averaging more than a mile thick, covers almost the entire continent. In a few places, the jagged tops of mountain ranges stick up through the ice, but most of Antarctica is a vast, smooth plateau of ice with an average elevation of 7,500 feet above sea level. The continent is lopsidedly centered on the South Pole and is divided into two contrasting parts—West Antarctica and East Antarctica—by the Transantarctic Mountains. This range stretches across the continent from the Weddell Sea to the Ross Sea.

Below: In summer the ice that covered the sea through the winter breaks up, littering the surface with wave-worn fragments.

A T L A N T I C

O C E A N

South Georgia

South
Orkney Is.

Falkland Is.

*Scotia
Sea*

ARGENTINA

CHILE

Deception I.

Graham
Land

Antarctic
Peninsula

Palmer
Archipelago

George V Sound

Alexander I.

Charcot I.

*Bellingshausen
Sea*

Peter I.

Ellsworth
Land

Thurston I.

*Amundsen
Sea*

Siple I.

S O U T H E R N   O C E A N

Coats Land

Dronning Maud Land

*Weddell
Sea*

Berkner I.

Ronne Ice
Shelf

Palmer Land

▲ Vinson Massif

W E S T

A N T A R C T I C A

Walgreen Coast

Transantarctic Mtns.

▲ Mt. Sidley

Mt. Kirkpatrick ▲

Mt. Markham ▲

● Marie Byrd
Land

Ross Ice
Shelf

Roosevelt I.

Mt. Erebus ▲

*Ross
Sea*

I N D I A N

O C E A N

Lützow-Holm Bay

Amundsen Bay

Enderby Land

Edward VIII Bay

Mac Robertson
Land

Prince Charles Mtns.

MacKenzie Bay

Amery Ice
Shelf

*Prydz
Bay*

E A S T

A N T A R C T I C A

SOUTH POLE
●

Amundsen-
Scott base

Queen Mary
Land

● Vostok
(Russia)

Victoria Land

Wilkes Land

Knox Coast

*Davis
Sea*

*Vincennes
Bay*

Dalton Ice Tongue

Porpoise Bay

Terre Adélie

Commonwealth Bay

Oates Land

Cook Ice Shelf

Sturge I.

Balleny Is.

P A C I F I C

O C E A N

Macquarie Is.

Campbell I.

Auckland I.

TASMANIA

Antipodes Is.

NEW ZEALAND

AUSTRALIA

0   1000   2000 Miles

0   1000   2000   3000 Km

Antarctica

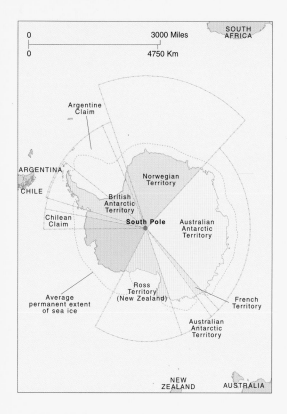

Above: After years of hunting that brought several whale species to the brink of extinction, Antarctica's whale populations are slowly recovering.

Left: Seven nations have set aside their territorial claims in Antarctica so that the continent can be used for peaceful scientific studies to benefit everyone.

Mountain ranges, basins, glaciers, and plateaus dominate West Antarctica. If the ice melted, this region would be a confusion of islands and seaways. West Antarctica reaches northward toward South America as a long, narrow S-shaped peninsula that is an extension of the Andes Mountains. Near the base of the peninsula, Vinson Massif, Antarctica's highest peak, rises to 16,860 feet. West Antarctica is much younger and more geologically active than East Antarctica is. Mount Erebus, Antarctica's most active volcano, occasionally spouts lava at the Ross Sea end of the Transantarctic range, and Deception Island near the tip of the peninsula erupted several times in the late 1960s.

East Antarctica is geologically much older. It is also much larger, covering almost three-fourths of the continent. A huge ice dome pushes up between the Transantarctic range and the mountains that rise along coastal sections of the Southern Ocean (sometimes also called the southern parts of the Indian and Atlantic Oceans). In the dome's center, the ice is more than 15,700 feet thick—deep enough to bury Chicago's Sears Tower 10 times over. In places, the weight of the ice has pressed the underlying land surface far below sea level. This enormous mass of ice contains 70 percent of the earth's fresh water.

Temperatures at the South Pole average -56°F and often fall below -90°F in the winter months. In 1983, scientists at Russia's Vostok Station, which sits 11,220 feet above sea level, recorded the world's lowest-ever air temperature of -128.6°F. High winds frequently sweep across the plateau and down the mountain slopes and glaciers of the peninsula. Winds of 70 miles per hour can blow for days at a time, but the windiest place on earth is Commonwealth Bay on the Antarctic Peninsula, where meteorologists have recorded gales of 200 miles per hour. Surprisingly, little new snow falls on Antarctica. Yearly total precipitation is about six inches—half the average for the Sahara Desert. The blizzards that often reduce visibility to a few yards are full of granular snow and ice grains that have been picked up, blown around, and dumped again, over and over.

Ice hides most of Antarctica's coastline, so maps generally show the outer limit of the permanent ice, including the huge **ice shelves** that partly fill the Ross Sea and the Weddell Sea. These shelves are up to 2,000 feet thick where they join the coast and 600 feet thick at their outer edge.

In summer, huge slabs break off and drift out to sea as **tabular icebergs.** One of the largest in recent years measured more than 200 miles long and 60 miles wide—an area almost as big as the states of Massachusetts and Connecticut combined. In winter the surface of the sea freezes, and thick **pack ice** extends up to 900 miles from the coast. In summer the ice breaks up into **ice floes** and wave-worn lumps called brash. Only at this time of year can supply ships reach the scientific stations around Antarctica's coast. The stations that are far inland, like Vostok and the U.S. Amundsen-Scott base at the South Pole, are supplied by air.

Only two kinds of flowering plants and tiny lichens, algae, and mosses manage to survive in Antarctica's harsh climate. Around the coast, penguins, skuas, petrels, and other seabirds arrive to breed in summer, and seals haul themselves onto ice floes and beaches to give birth to their pups. By contrast, the Southern Ocean teems with life. Plankton (tiny floating plants and animals) and their larger relatives, the shrimplike krill, feed fish and **baleen** whales. Fish and squid, in turn, provide food for seals and toothed whales.

Geologists have found copper, manganese, zinc, chromium, lead, and other minerals in Antarctica, as well as thick coal seams exposed in cliff faces in the Transantarctic Mountains. But any such mining is forbidden under the Antarctic Treaty. Oil and gas fields may lie beneath the continental shelves around Antarctica and its fringing islands, but these, too, are out of reach.

Antarctica's value to humans does not lie in a few hard-to-reach resources but in its value as a unique natural laboratory. Atmospheric scientists working in Antarctica first alerted the world to the hole in the ozone layer—the thin veil of ozone gas that protects the earth from damaging radiation from the sun. That discovery led to research into the cause of the problem—and to international agreements to phase out the industrial chemicals, called CFCs, that were found to be causing most of the damage. Glaciologists examine patterns of ice movement and the effects of global warming on the Antarctic ice sheets. Biologists study the sea and land life, including fish that have developed a natural antifreeze to prevent them from freezing in the icy sea. These and other studies continue to add to our understanding of the natural environment.

Below: Adélie penguins dive into the water to hunt for fish.

Glossary

archipelago: a group of islands that stretches across a sea or ocean

atoll: a ring-shaped coral reef that encloses a lagoon (a stretch of seawater)

baleen: the rows of thin, flexible strips in the jaw of a toothless whale that allow it to sift small animals out of seawater

British Commonwealth: a free association of sovereign states, consisting of Britain and some of its former colonies and dependencies

cassava: a plant grown in the tropics that has a fleshy edible root whose starch is a source of nutrition

colony: a territory ruled by another power that is typically located far away

copra: the dried meat of the coconut that can be processed into coconut oil

coral reef: a ridge of rocklike formations made up of billions of coral polyp skeletons

federal: relating to a type of government in which states or groups unite under a central power. The states or groups surrender power to make some decisions but retain limited territorial control.

geothermal power: energy produced by the heat of the earth's interior

geyser: an underground spring that, from time to time, throws up jets of heated water and steam

global warming: an increase in the earth's average temperature that may be caused by the sun's heat becoming trapped in the atmosphere by certain gases

ice floe: a thick, flat piece of floating ice that has broken off from an ice shelf

ice shelf: a large, thick piece of floating ice that is attached to a coastline

League of Nations: an international organization formed after World War I (1914–1918)

Maori: a member of the Polynesian people who are native to New Zealand

outback: the isolated rural section of central Australia

pack ice: blocks of ice that form on the surface of the sea and that often are broken into pieces by wind or currents

plateau: a large, relatively flat area that stands above the surrounding land

protectorate: a territory under the authority of another

tabular iceberg: a large, flat-topped, rectangular piece of ice that has broken off from an ice shelf

taro: a plant grown throughout the tropics that has edible, starchy rootstocks

tropical rain forest: a dense, green forest that receives large amounts of rain every year. These forests lie near the equator.

Tropic of Capricorn: an imaginary circle around the earth that parallels the equator to the south. The Tropic of Cancer parallels the equator to the north. The hot, humid area between the two circles is called the tropics.

trust territory: a non-self-governing territory placed under the temporary authority of a nation by the United Nations

United Nations: an organization of nations formed after World War II (1939–1945) that works toward world peace and the betterment of humanity

Index